Curriculum Visions

Move on with Dividing

Curriculum Visions

There's much more online including videos

You will find multimedia resources covering a wide range of topics at:

www.CurriculumVisions.com

CurriculumVisions is a subscription web site.

A CVP Book

Series Concept
Brian Knapp, BSc, PhD

Text contributed by
Brian Knapp, BSc, PhD, and Colin Bass, BSc, MA

Editors
Lorna Gilbert, Barbara Carragher, and Gillian Gatehouse

Senior Designer
Adele Humphries, BA, PGCE

Illustrations
David Woodroffe

Designed and produced by
Atlantic Europe Publishing

Printed in China by
WKT Company Ltd

Curriculum Visions Move on with Maths – Dividing
A CIP record for this book is available from the British Library

ISBN: 978 1 86214 558 0

Picture credits
All photographs are from the Earthscape Picture Library and ShutterStock collections.

This product is manufactured from sustainable managed forests. For every tree cut down at least one more is planted.

Move on with Maths Resources CD

You will find hundreds of photocopiable word problems in the teacher's 'Move on with Maths Resources CD', which is available for separate purchase.

Look out for these sections to help you learn more about each topic:

Remember... This provides a summary of the key concept(s) on each two-page entry. Use it to revise what you have learned.

Can you do this? These problems reinforce the concepts learned on a particular spread, and can be used to test existing knowledge.

Answers to the problems set in the 'Move on with Maths' series can be found at: **www.curriculumvisions.com/moveOnAnswers**

Place value

To make it easy for you to see exactly what we are doing, you will find coloured columns behind the numbers in all the examples on this and the following pages. This is what the colours mean:

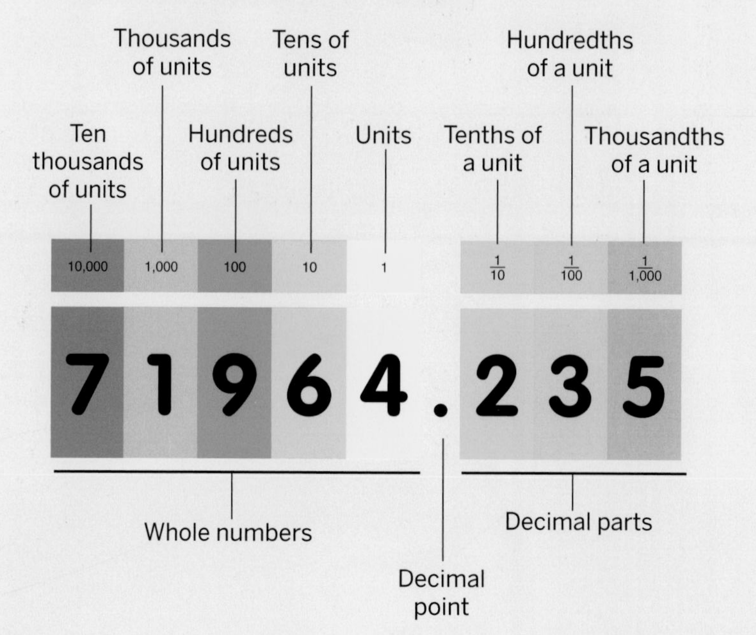

Contents

Why divide?

Division is a way of sharing, by quickly taking away, or subtracting, the same number again and again.

How many times 10 can be shared into 2's?

Subtracting **2** from **10** is one way to find out. Start with **10** and subtract **2**. You are left with **8**. Then start with **8** and subtract **2** and so on until you come to **0**.

This takes **5** subtractions. So simply by subtracting, we know that **10** can be shared into **5** lots of **2**.

$$10 - 2 = 8$$
$$8 - 2 = 6$$
$$6 - 2 = 4$$
$$4 - 2 = 2$$
$$2 - 2 = 0$$

Counting diamonds

A jeweller buys a bag of **84** diamonds, all of equal size. He wants to make brooches that each use **7** diamonds in a gold mounting.

However, unless he knows how many gold mountings he will need, he is in danger of buying too many and wasting his money. Or he might buy too few and have to go back to the warehouse to buy more, so wasting his time.

The jeweller decides to divide up the diamonds into little piles, each containing **7** jewels. What he is doing is subtracting **7** jewels from the main collection and setting them aside. Then he subtracts **7** more from the remaining collection and sets those aside. And so on. This takes him a long time. He would have been better off using dividing.

$$84 - 7 = 77$$
$$77 - 7 = 70$$
$$70 - 7 = 63$$
$$63 - 7 = 56$$
$$56 - 7 = 49$$
$$49 - 7 = 42$$
$$42 - 7 = 35$$
$$35 - 7 = 28$$
$$28 - 7 = 21$$
$$21 - 7 = 14$$
$$14 - 7 = 7$$
$$7 - 7 = 0$$

Grandpa is deciding who will have his money after he dies. He is making a Will. After he has decided how much money to leave to other people, he has **£30,433** left to share equally between his **13** grandchildren. He wants to work out how much they each receive.

He thinks of going to a bank to collect **30,433** pound coins, in order to count out piles like the jeweller did. That does not seem a good idea.

Instead, he takes **30** slips of white paper and writes **£1,000** on each one. He shares them into **13** piles, one for each grandchild.

30 – 13 = 17 Each grandchild will receive **£1,000** so far.

17 – 13 = 4 Each grandchild will receive **£2,000** so far.

He has **4** slips of white paper, standing for **£4,000**, left over. He also has **£433** he did not think about before.

He changes to slips of yellow paper, and writes **£100** on each one.

He needs **40** of these to exchange for the **4** white **£1,000** slips left over, and **4** more for **£400** from the **£433**, that is **40 + 4 = 44** slips of yellow paper. He shares them onto the same **13** piles.

44 – 13 = 31 **31 – 13 = 18** **18 – 13 = 5**

Each grandchild will receive **£2,300** so far.

Grandpa exchanges the **5** yellow slips left over for **50** green slips labelled **£10**. He needs another **3** for the **£30** from the **£33** he put on one side before. Altogether, he needs **50 + 3 = 53**. He shares them onto the same **13** piles.

53 – 13 = 40 **40 – 13 = 27** **27 – 13 = 14** **14 – 13 = 1**

Each grandchild will receive **£2,340** so far.

The one remaining **£10** slip plus the odd **£3** makes **£13**, enough for each child to have another pound, with nothing left over.

Each grandchild will receive **£2,341**.

Grandpa could have reached the same answer more quickly by dividing, as you will see on the following pages.

Remember... When you repeat subtraction, you take away the same number time after time. Division is a short way of doing this, but only if the number you are subtracting is the same time after time.

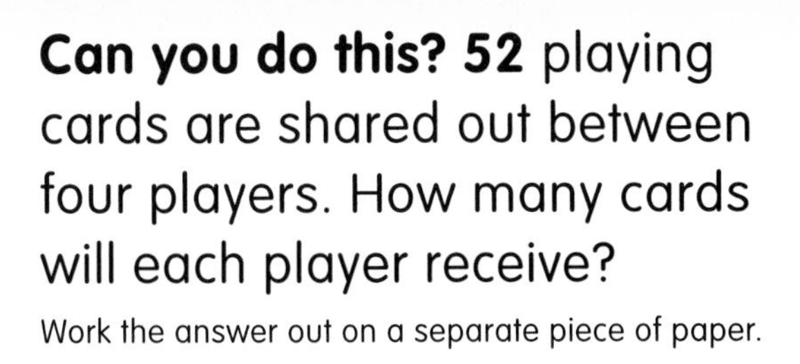

Can you do this? 52 playing cards are shared out between four players. How many cards will each player receive?

Work the answer out on a separate piece of paper.

Sharing

Sharing a collection of things is a way of dividing to give out a collection in equal parts.

Strawberry-fest

Frank was very proud of the organic strawberries he grew in his back garden. In summer he and his wife Elsie often had a bowl of them with cream. They were very fair about it. Elsie used to share the strawberries out equally for them into bowls, saying: "One for you, one for me, one for you, one for me..." until they had enough – usually about **12** each.

One Sunday, Frank and Elsie's children came over, bringing Frank's mother too. As there would be **7** people, Frank would need to pick more strawberries than usual. He didn't count them, he just picked what he thought would be enough. He picked **84**.

But he could have worked out just what he needed before he went to pick the fruit. Sharing things out equally is one of the useful things you can do quickly using dividing,

84 =

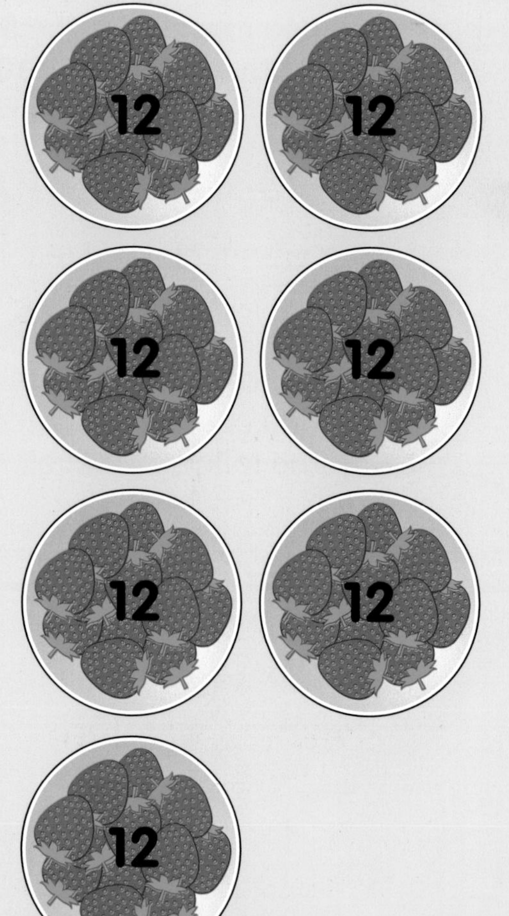

Further example

Frank could have done that quickly using the **7** times table backwards.

$$7 \times 12 = 84$$

Here is another use for multiplying facts.

Frank and Elsie were not sure whether Elsie's parents would come for strawberries also. If they did, there would be **9** people there. Frank wanted to be sure the strawberries could be shared out equally between either **7** or **9** people.

He worked out he should pick **63** strawberries, because

7 x 9 = 63
(7 people, 9 strawberries each)

and

9 x 7 = 63
(9 people, 7 strawberries each)

Remember... Sharing equally is separating out – or dividing out – a number into many equal parts. So it is a form of division.

Can you do this? The jeweller on page 4 made **12** brooches with **7** diamonds in each. On page 6, Frank filled **7** dishes with **12** strawberries in each.
Can you write down, on a separate piece of paper, how the Turn-Around Rule for multiplying links these two problems?
(Hint: see pages 14–15)

How dividing works

Here is a model to show what happens when you divide.

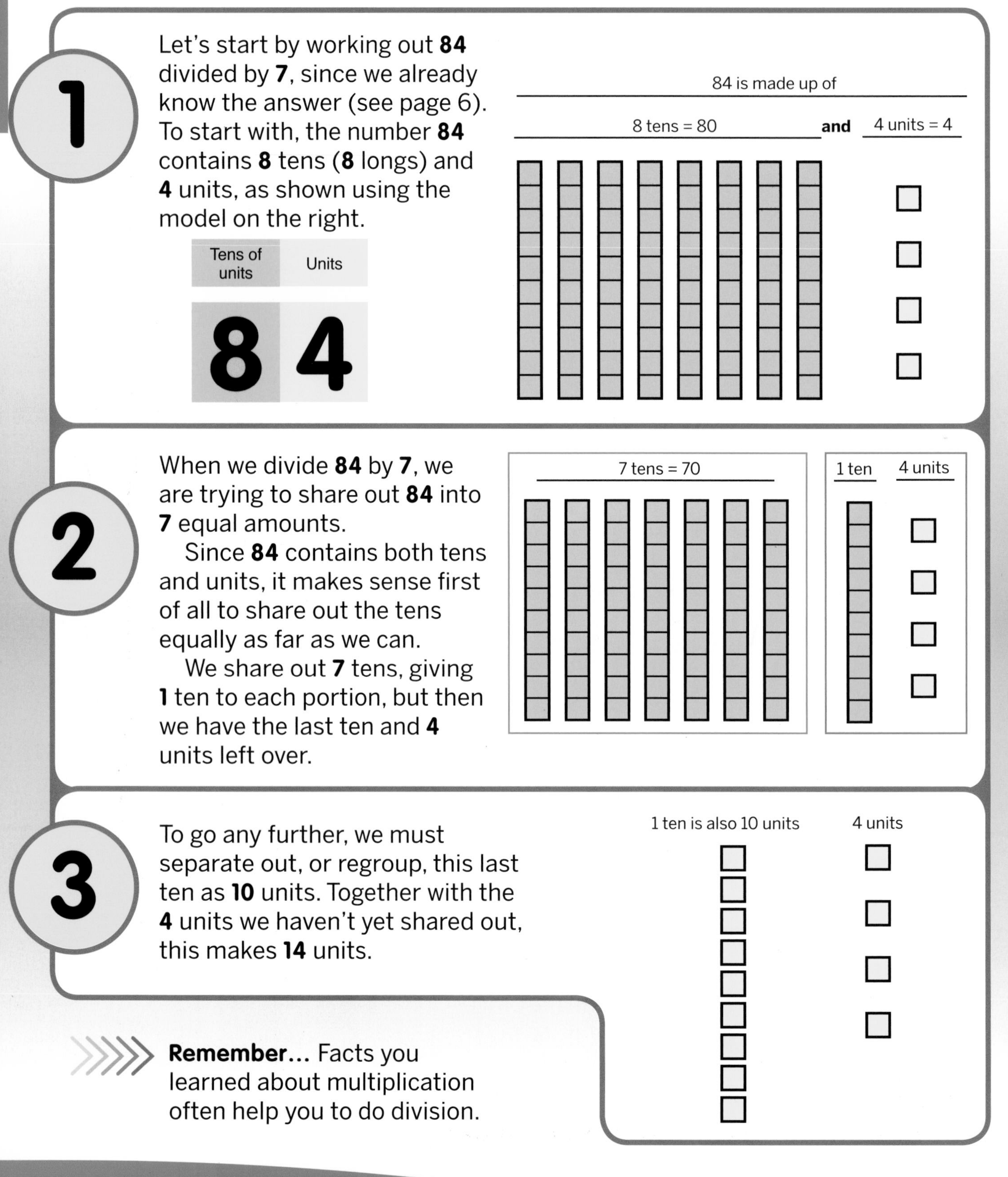

1

Let's start by working out **84** divided by **7**, since we already know the answer (see page 6). To start with, the number **84** contains **8** tens (**8** longs) and **4** units, as shown using the model on the right.

2

When we divide **84** by **7**, we are trying to share out **84** into **7** equal amounts.

Since **84** contains both tens and units, it makes sense first of all to share out the tens equally as far as we can.

We share out **7** tens, giving **1** ten to each portion, but then we have the last ten and **4** units left over.

3

To go any further, we must separate out, or regroup, this last ten as **10** units. Together with the **4** units we haven't yet shared out, this makes **14** units.

Remember... Facts you learned about multiplication often help you to do division.

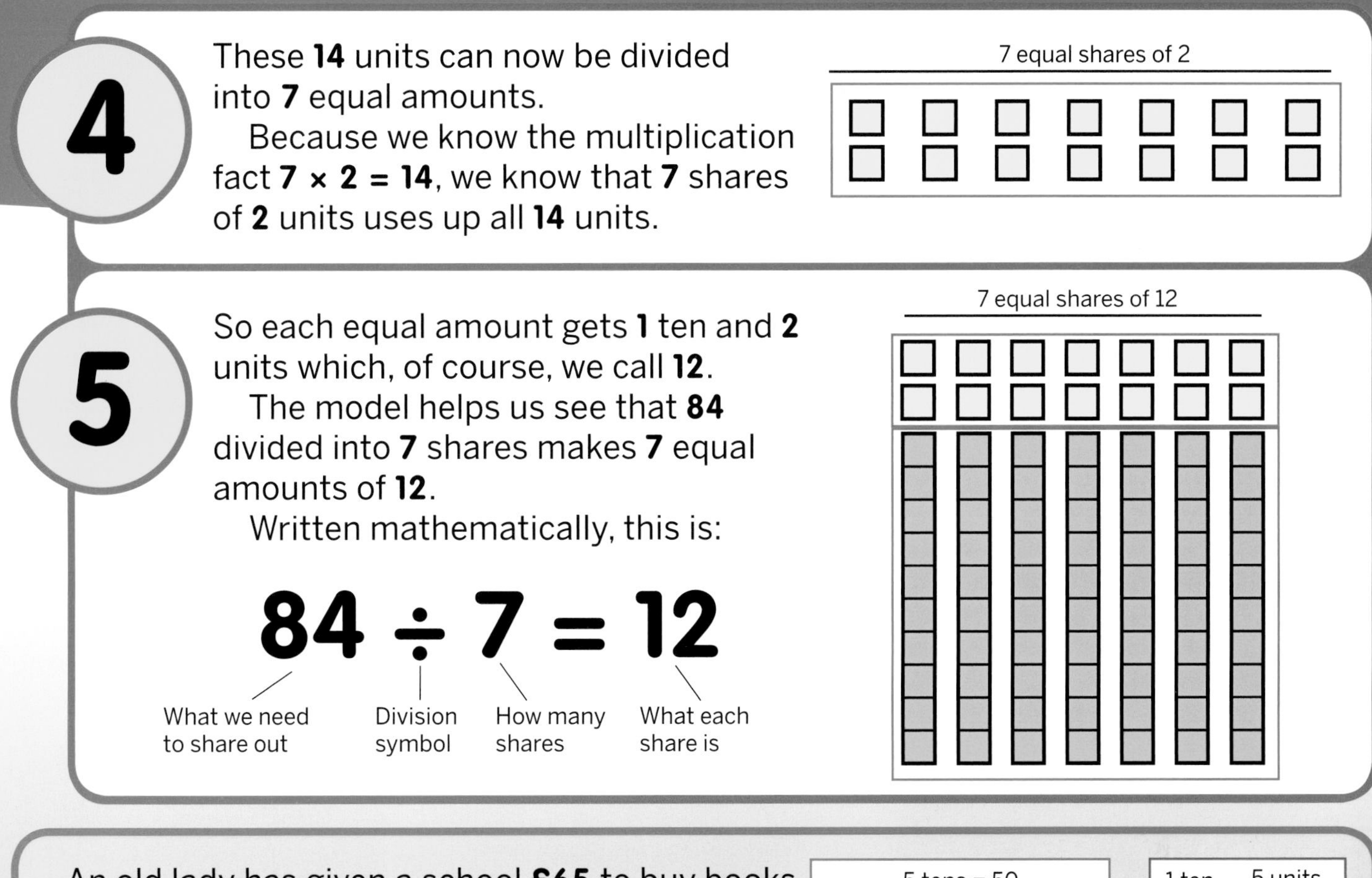

4

These **14** units can now be divided into **7** equal amounts.

Because we know the multiplication fact **7 × 2 = 14**, we know that **7** shares of **2** units uses up all **14** units.

5

So each equal amount gets **1** ten and **2** units which, of course, we call **12**.

The model helps us see that **84** divided into **7** shares makes **7** equal amounts of **12**.

Written mathematically, this is:

$$84 \div 7 = 12$$

What we need to share out — Division symbol — How many shares — What each share is

An old lady has given a school **£65** to buy books for the child with the best attendance record. Five children have equally good attendance records, and they have to share the prize. How much can be spent on each one?

6 longs + 5 units =
5 longs + (1 long + 5 units) =
5 longs + 15 units

5 tens = 50

1 ten — 5 units

5 equal shares of 13

Shared between five, each child receives **1** long **+ 3** units (using multiplication fact **15 = 5 x 3**).

That is, **65** shared between **5 = 13**.

$$65 \div 5 = 13$$

Can you do this? On a separate piece of paper, draw diagrams of longs and units to show how the 52 cards on page 5 were shared between four players.
When you did it before, did you use this quicker method, or did you deal them out one at a time as you do when playing cards?

Short division

If you want to divide by a number smaller than 10 you use short division.

As an example we will use the same calculation as on the previous page: **84** divided by **7**. You can then compare the short division method with the model method we used on page 8.

The number we need to share out

Shares

84 ÷ 7 = ?

Division symbol

The answer we are going to calculate!

1

For short division we begin by writing the shares (**7**) and the total (**84**) side by side.

A half bracket is placed between the two numbers and a line put below the number we need to share out. The answer will go below the line.

Notice that we have used coloured columns to help us to separate the tens from the units.

Half bracket

Shares

Tens	Units
8	4
?	?

7)84

Line goes below the number we need to share out

The result of the calculation will be written below the line

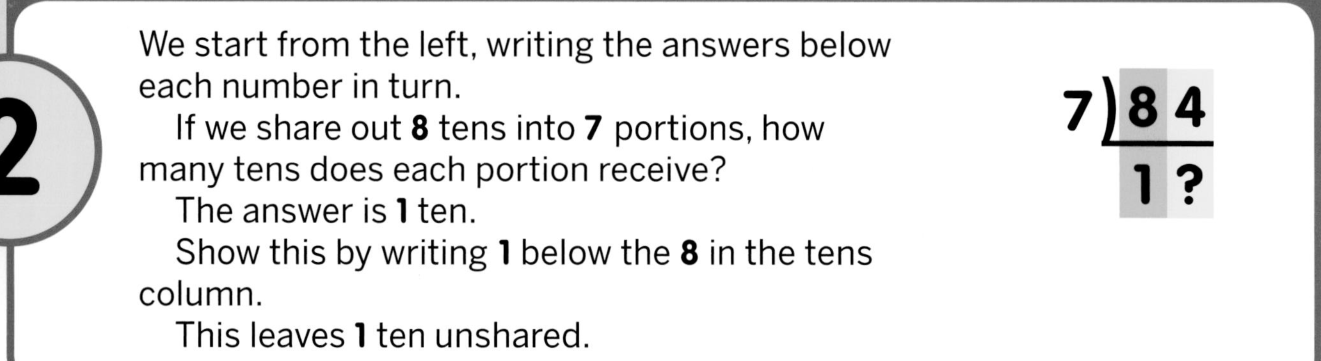

2

We start from the left, writing the answers below each number in turn.

If we share out **8** tens into **7** portions, how many tens does each portion receive?

The answer is **1** ten.

Show this by writing **1** below the **8** in the tens column.

This leaves **1** ten unshared.

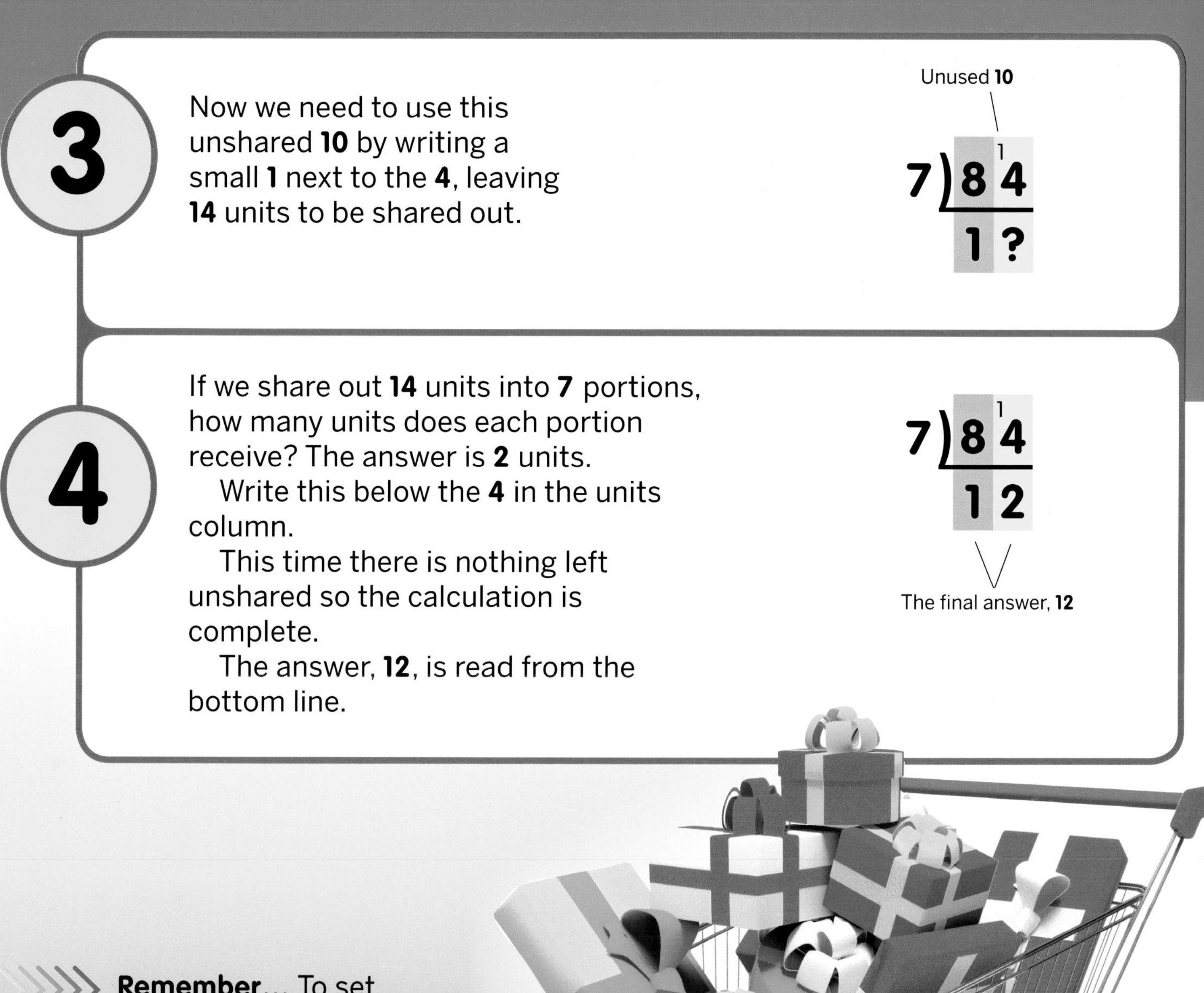

3

Now we need to use this unshared **10** by writing a small **1** next to the **4**, leaving **14** units to be shared out.

4

If we share out **14** units into **7** portions, how many units does each portion receive? The answer is **2** units.

Write this below the **4** in the units column.

This time there is nothing left unshared so the calculation is complete.

The answer, **12**, is read from the bottom line.

Remember... To set out numbers for short division, put the number you are dividing with first, then a half bracket, then the number you are dividing into. Then start dividing from the left.

Can you do these?

48 ÷ 3 = ?

56 ÷ 4 = ?

80 ÷ 5 = ?

Work the answers out on a separate piece of paper.

More short division

Short division can be used on large numbers if you are still dividing by a number less than 10.

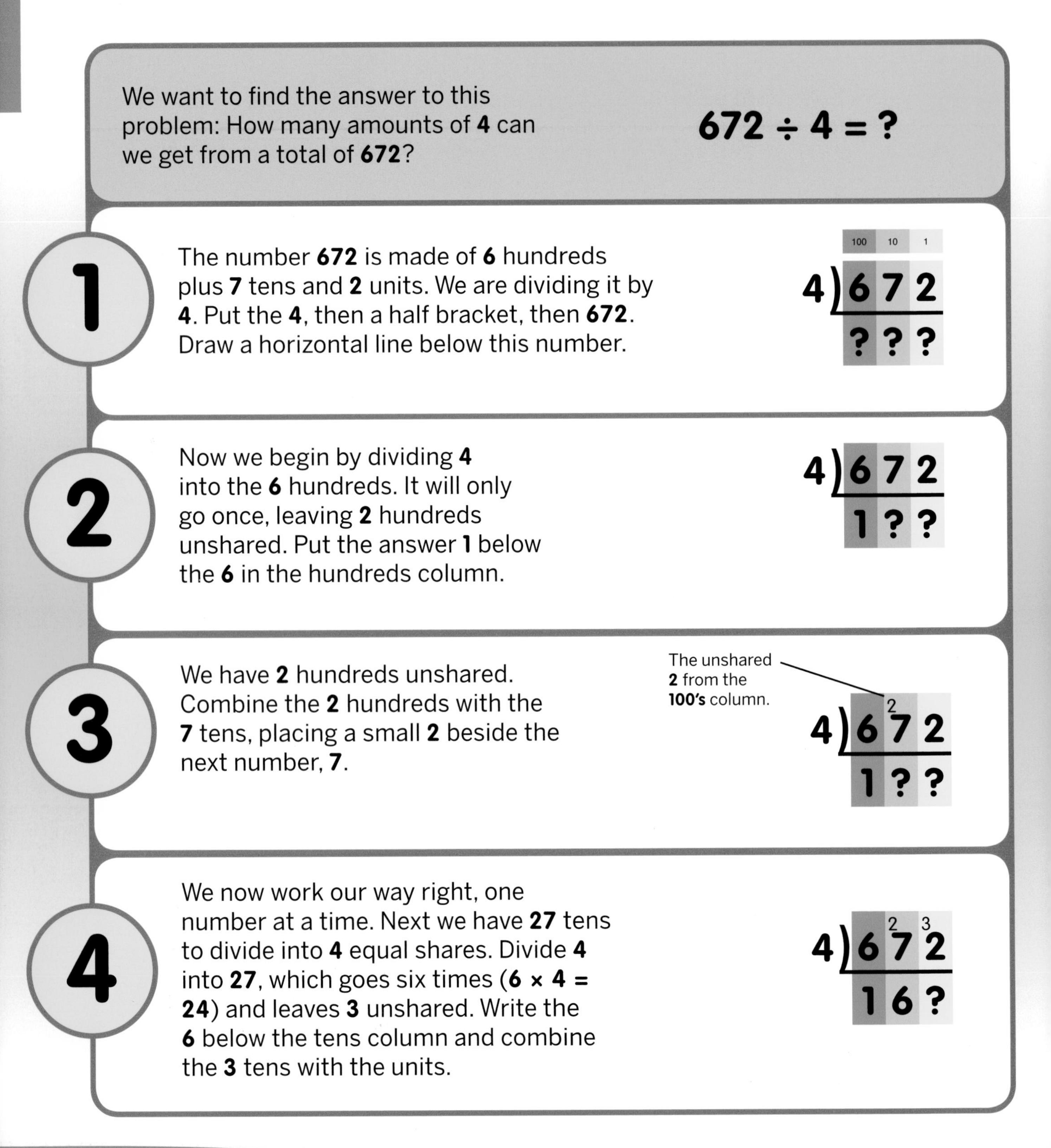

We want to find the answer to this problem: How many amounts of **4** can we get from a total of **672**?

672 ÷ 4 = ?

1 The number **672** is made of **6** hundreds plus **7** tens and **2** units. We are dividing it by **4**. Put the **4**, then a half bracket, then **672**. Draw a horizontal line below this number.

2 Now we begin by dividing **4** into the **6** hundreds. It will only go once, leaving **2** hundreds unshared. Put the answer **1** below the **6** in the hundreds column.

3 We have **2** hundreds unshared. Combine the **2** hundreds with the **7** tens, placing a small **2** beside the next number, **7**.

4 We now work our way right, one number at a time. Next we have **27** tens to divide into **4** equal shares. Divide **4** into **27**, which goes six times (**6 × 4 = 24**) and leaves **3** unshared. Write the **6** below the tens column and combine the **3** tens with the units.

5

Now we work one place right again, into the units column. We have **32** units to be divided into **4** equal shares. The answer is **8** exactly. Place **8** under the **2**.

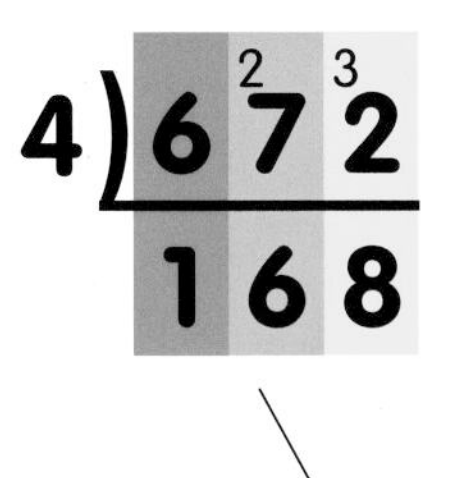

The final answer, **168**

672 ÷ 4 = 168

The final answer, **168**, is read from the bottom line.

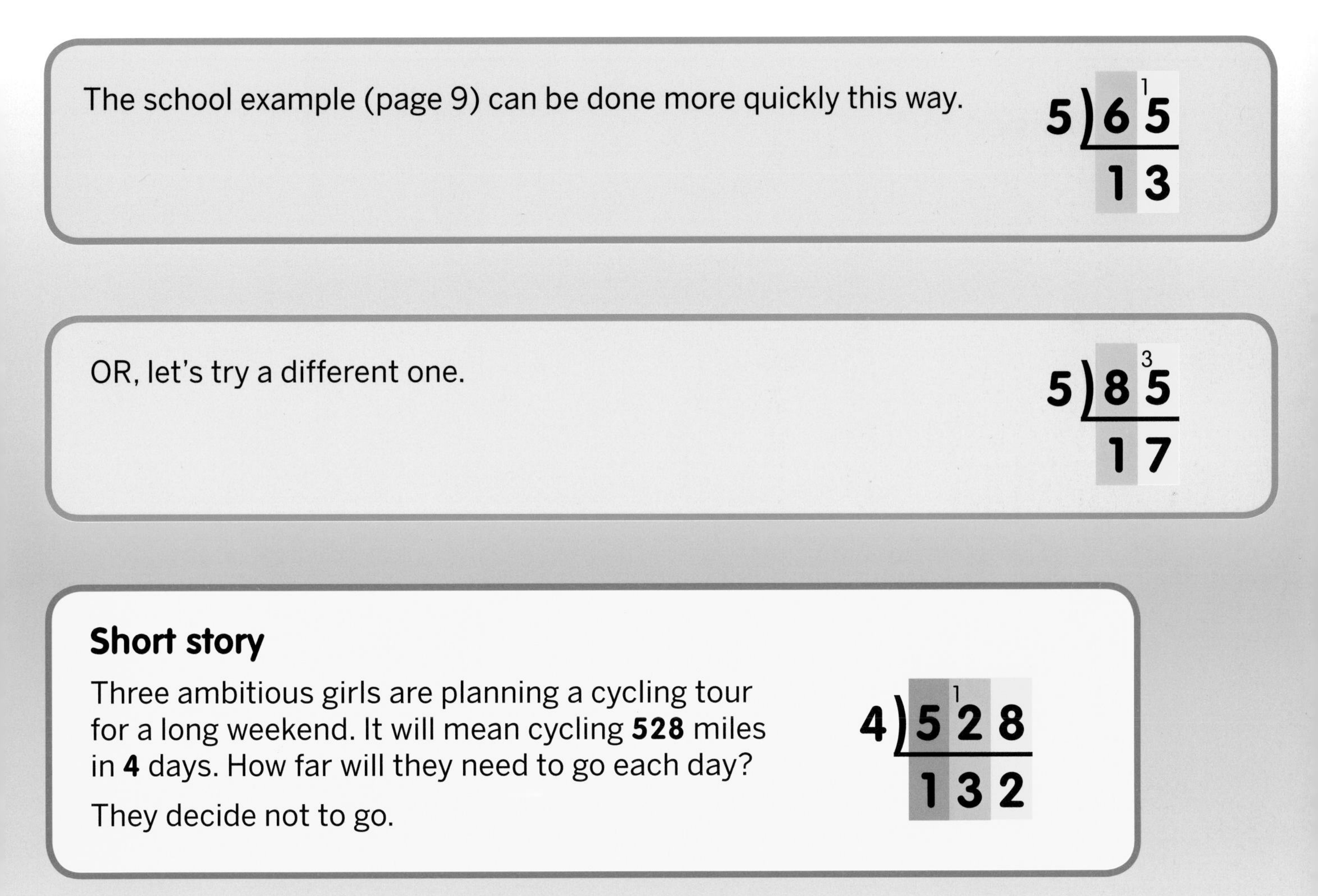

The school example (page 9) can be done more quickly this way.

5)6 ¹5
1 3

OR, let's try a different one.

5)8 ³5
1 7

Short story

Three ambitious girls are planning a cycling tour for a long weekend. It will mean cycling **528** miles in **4** days. How far will they need to go each day?

They decide not to go.

4)5 ¹2 8
1 3 2

Can you do these?

585 ÷ 5 = ?

672 ÷ 6 = ?

833 ÷ 7 = ?

Work the answers out on a separate piece of paper.

Remember... Draw a line under the larger number and divide from left to right. Put the answers below the line.

Division and multiplication

Division and multiplication are very closely related. We can use a multiplication square to divide!

Multiplication fact

Division fact

For every one multiplication fact, there are two division facts.

Division fact

Using a multiplication square

You can make use of a multiplication square to divide because division is multiplication backwards.

Let's take the multiplication fact that we have used on pages 4 and 6 again:

$$7 \times 12 = 84$$

We know that **84** shared out equally **7** times makes **12**.

Using ÷ as the symbol for 'divided by' and **=** for 'makes' this word sentence can be written as an equation:

$$84 \div 7 = 12$$

See how the numbers have changed sides from the multiplication equation?

We can look at the numbers in yet another way:

$$84 \div 12 = 7$$

Each multiplication fact has two division facts connected to it. The number square at the top of the opposite page shows this clearly.

Division fact 1

$84 \div 7 = 12$

Division fact 2

$84 \div 12 = 7$

Multiplication fact

$7 \times 12 = 84$

×	1	2	3	4	5	6	7	8	9	10	11	12
1	1	2	3	4	5	6	7	8	9	10	11	12
2	2	4	6	8	10	12	14	16	18	20	22	24
3	3	6	9	12	15	18	21	24	27	30	33	36
4	4	8	12	16	20	24	28	32	36	40	44	48
5	5	10	15	20	25	30	35	40	45	50	55	60
6	6	12	18	24	30	36	42	48	54	60	66	72
7	7	14	21	28	35	42	49	56	63	70	77	84
8	8	16	24	32	40	48	56	64	72	80	88	96
9	9	18	27	36	45	54	63	72	81	90	99	108
10	10	20	30	40	50	60	70	80	90	100	110	120
11	11	22	33	44	55	66	77	88	99	110	121	132
12	12	24	36	48	60	72	84	96	108	120	132	144

Here is another example: The multiplication fact **$4 \times 6 = 24$** is connected to the two division facts **$24 \div 6 = 4$** and **$24 \div 4 = 6$**.

Division fact 1

$24 \div 6 = 4$

Division fact 2

$24 \div 4 = 6$

Multiplication fact

$4 \times 6 = 24$

×	1	2	3	4	5	6	7	8	9	10	11	12
1	1	2	3	4	5	6	7	8	9	10	11	12
2	2	4	6	8	10	12	14	16	18	20	22	24
3	3	6	9	12	15	18	21	24	27	30	33	36
4	4	8	12	16	20	24	28	32	36	40	44	48
5	5	10	15	20	25	30	35	40	45	50	55	60
6	6	12	18	24	30	36	42	48	54	60	66	72
7	7	14	21	28	35	42	49	56	63	70	77	84
8	8	16	24	32	40	48	56	64	72	80	88	96
9	9	18	27	36	45	54	63	72	81	90	99	108
10	10	20	30	40	50	60	70	80	90	100	110	120
11	11	22	33	44	55	66	77	88	99	110	121	132
12	12	24	36	48	60	72	84	96	108	120	132	144

Can you do these?

$15 \div 3 = ?$

$15 \div 5 = ?$

$66 \div 11 = ?$

$66 \div 6 = ?$

$121 \div 11 = ?$

Work the answers out on a separate piece of paper.

Which multiplication fact did you use each time?

Remember... Every multiplication fact is connected to two division facts simply by rearranging the equation.

Long division

Long division is a way of dividing when the number you are dividing by is bigger than 10.

Suppose we have to divide **783** by **27**.

$$783 \div 27 = ?$$

1

Write down the numbers as shown here. It is much the same as for short division, but notice that the line goes above the number and the answer builds on top of that. This is because the space underneath is needed for the working.

	100	10	1
	?	**?**	**?**
27)	**7**	**8**	**3**

2

Start on the left.

How many times can we divide **27** into **7**? Answer **0**, because **27** is bigger than **7**.
We do not need to write this **0** down and instead leave a blank.

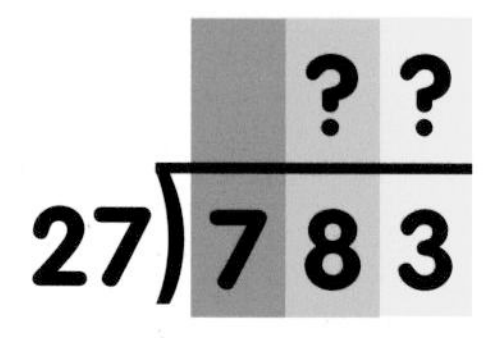

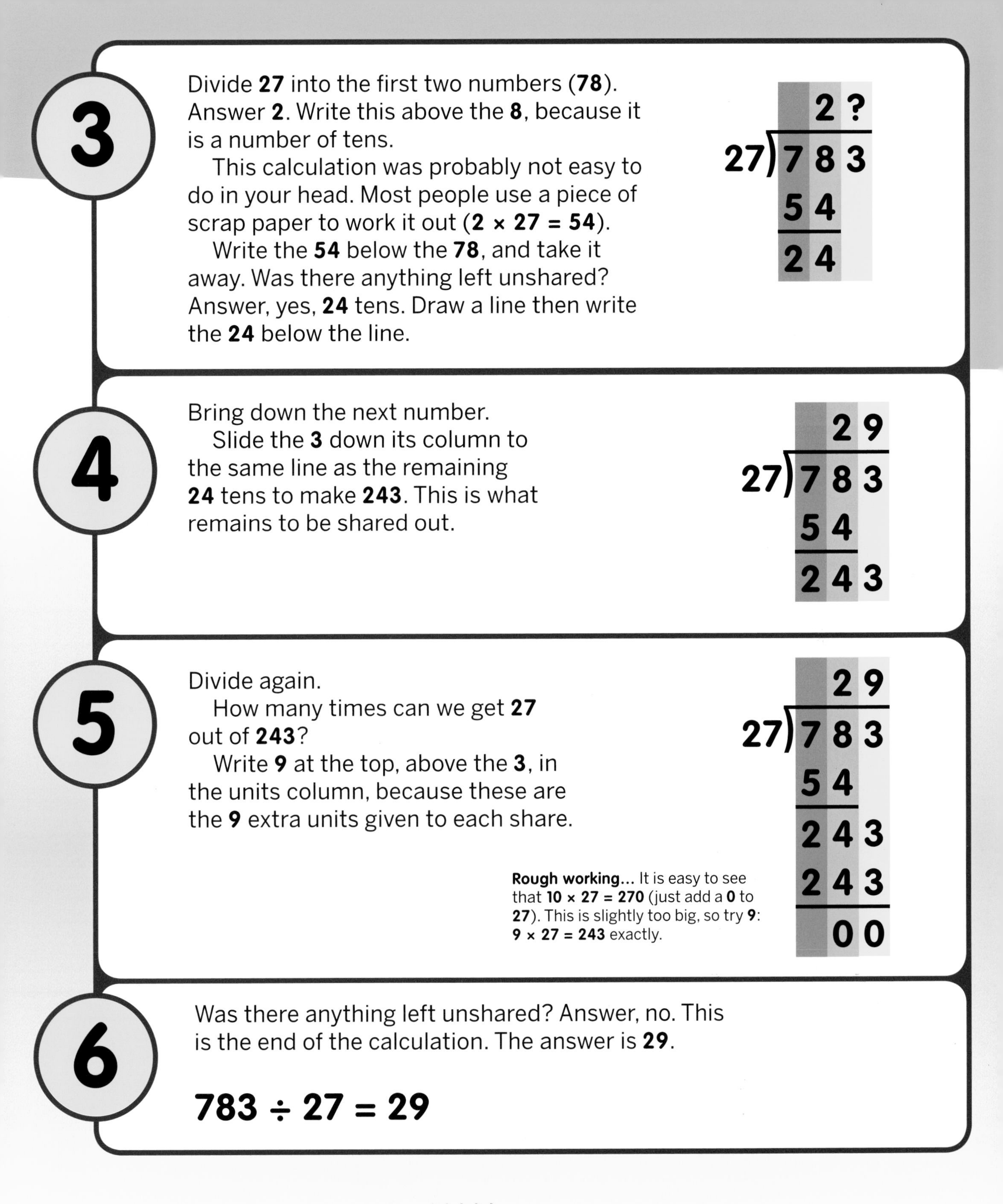

3

Divide **27** into the first two numbers (**78**). Answer **2**. Write this above the **8**, because it is a number of tens.

This calculation was probably not easy to do in your head. Most people use a piece of scrap paper to work it out (**2 × 27 = 54**).

Write the **54** below the **78**, and take it away. Was there anything left unshared? Answer, yes, **24** tens. Draw a line then write the **24** below the line.

4

Bring down the next number.

Slide the **3** down its column to the same line as the remaining **24** tens to make **243**. This is what remains to be shared out.

5

Divide again.

How many times can we get **27** out of **243**?

Write **9** at the top, above the **3**, in the units column, because these are the **9** extra units given to each share.

Rough working... It is easy to see that **10 × 27 = 270** (just add a **0** to **27**). This is slightly too big, so try **9**: **9 × 27 = 243** exactly.

6

Was there anything left unshared? Answer, no. This is the end of the calculation. The answer is **29**.

783 ÷ 27 = 29

Can you do these?

629 ÷ 17 = ?

361 ÷ 19 = ?

Work the answers out on a separate piece of paper.

Remember... Short division and long division are just the same. They are simply different ways of writing down division.

Quick division tips

Here are tips for knowing what to expect in your answer.

When we are deciding which division method to use, it is often helpful to know in advance whether the division will work out exactly, or whether there will be some left over. If it will work out exactly, we can often use short division or do the sum in our heads. If it won't go exactly, we might have to use a calculator, or do it by long division if there is no calculator handy.

Here are some easy tests to find out.

9 If a number divides by **9**, the sum of its digits divides by **9**. Example: **7,128**; the sum of the digits is **7 + 1 + 2 + 8 = 18**, and **18 ÷ 9 = 2**, so **7,128** divides by **9**.

5 If a number divides by **5**, its last digit is **5** or **0**. Example: **70** ends in a **0** and **695** ends in a **5**, so they both divide by **5**.

10 If a number divides by **10**, its last digit is **0**. Example: The number **3,420** ends in a **0** and so divides by **10**.

8 If a number divides by **8**, the number formed by its last three digits divides by **8**. Example: **6,128**; the last three digits are **128** and **128 ÷ 8 = 16**, so **6,128** divides by **8**.

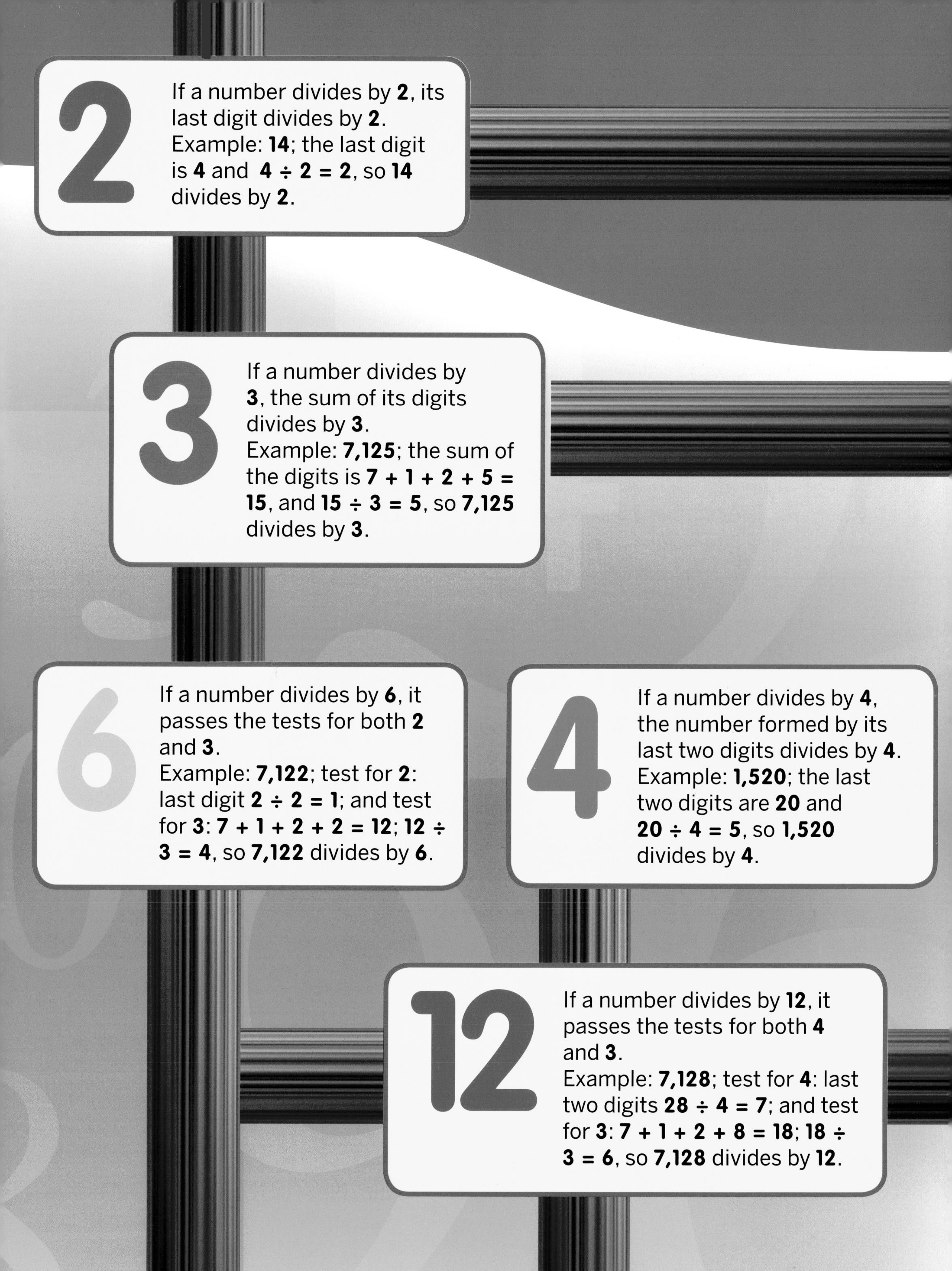

2

If a number divides by **2**, its last digit divides by **2**. Example: **14**; the last digit is **4** and **4 ÷ 2 = 2**, so **14** divides by **2**.

3

If a number divides by **3**, the sum of its digits divides by **3**. Example: **7,125**; the sum of the digits is **7 + 1 + 2 + 5 = 15**, and **15 ÷ 3 = 5**, so **7,125** divides by **3**.

6

If a number divides by **6**, it passes the tests for both **2** and **3**. Example: **7,122**; test for **2**: last digit **2 ÷ 2 = 1**; and test for **3**: **7 + 1 + 2 + 2 = 12**; **12 ÷ 3 = 4**, so **7,122** divides by **6**.

4

If a number divides by **4**, the number formed by its last two digits divides by **4**. Example: **1,520**; the last two digits are **20** and **20 ÷ 4 = 5**, so **1,520** divides by **4**.

12

If a number divides by **12**, it passes the tests for both **4** and **3**. Example: **7,128**; test for **4**: last two digits **28 ÷ 4 = 7**; and test for **3**: **7 + 1 + 2 + 8 = 18**; **18 ÷ 3 = 6**, so **7,128** divides by **12**.

Remainders

When division leaves something over, the amount left over is called a remainder.

Suppose we want to divide **78** by **4**.

78 ÷ 4 = ?

1

We will use short division because we are dividing by a number smaller than **10**.

The number **78** is made up of **7** tens and **8** units.

Find out how many times you can get **4** out of **7**. Put the answer **1** below the **7**. There is a remainder to carry forward of **3**.

	10	1
4)	7	8
	1	?

The answer appears on the bottom line

2

The **3** left over is in the tens column, so it is worth **30** units. This, together with the **8** we haven't used yet, can be combined into **30 + 8 = 38** to be shared out.

4)	7	³8
	1	?

This is the number carried forward

3

How many times can you get **4** out of **38**? Answer **9** times, because **4 × 9 = 36**. Put the **9** below the **38**. Now there is just **2** left over. We cannot share **2** out equally between **4**. The left-over amount is called the remainder.

4)	7	³8
	1	9

remainder 2

Remember... A remainder occurs in division when the original number cannot be shared out equally.

Another example: What is the remainder when you divide **654** by **9**?

654 ÷ 9 = ?

1

Divide **9** into **6**. It won't go. Carry the **6** to the right.

100	10	1
6	5	4
	?	?

2

Divide **9** into **65** (**9 × 7 = 63**). Put **7** below the **5**. Carry the remainder of **2** to the right.

6	5	^{2}4
	7	?

3

Divide **9** into **24** (**9 × 2 = 18**). Put **2** below the **4**. The remainder is **6**.

So the answer is **72**, remainder **6**. This can be written as the mixed number **72** $\frac{6}{9}$ and simplified to **72** $\frac{2}{3}$.

6	5	^{2}4
	7	2

remainder 6

Sometimes remainders can be shared further, for example **$13** shared between **4** American children gives **3** dollars and a quarter each. This could be written as a decimal, **$3.25**. Sometimes it does not work out exactly. **£13** shared between **3** British children gives either **£4** each and **£1** left over; or **£4.33** each and **1** penny left over. Sometimes the remainder can be saved for future use. Sometimes it is wasted.

Can you do these? What is the remainder in each of these?

38 ÷ 3 = ? **102 ÷ 4 = ?** **341 ÷ 5 = ?**

Work the answers out on a separate piece of paper.

Now you have worked out the answers, look back at the previous page to see if you can find quicker ways to work them out.

Remainders in long division

Long divisions often leave remainders.

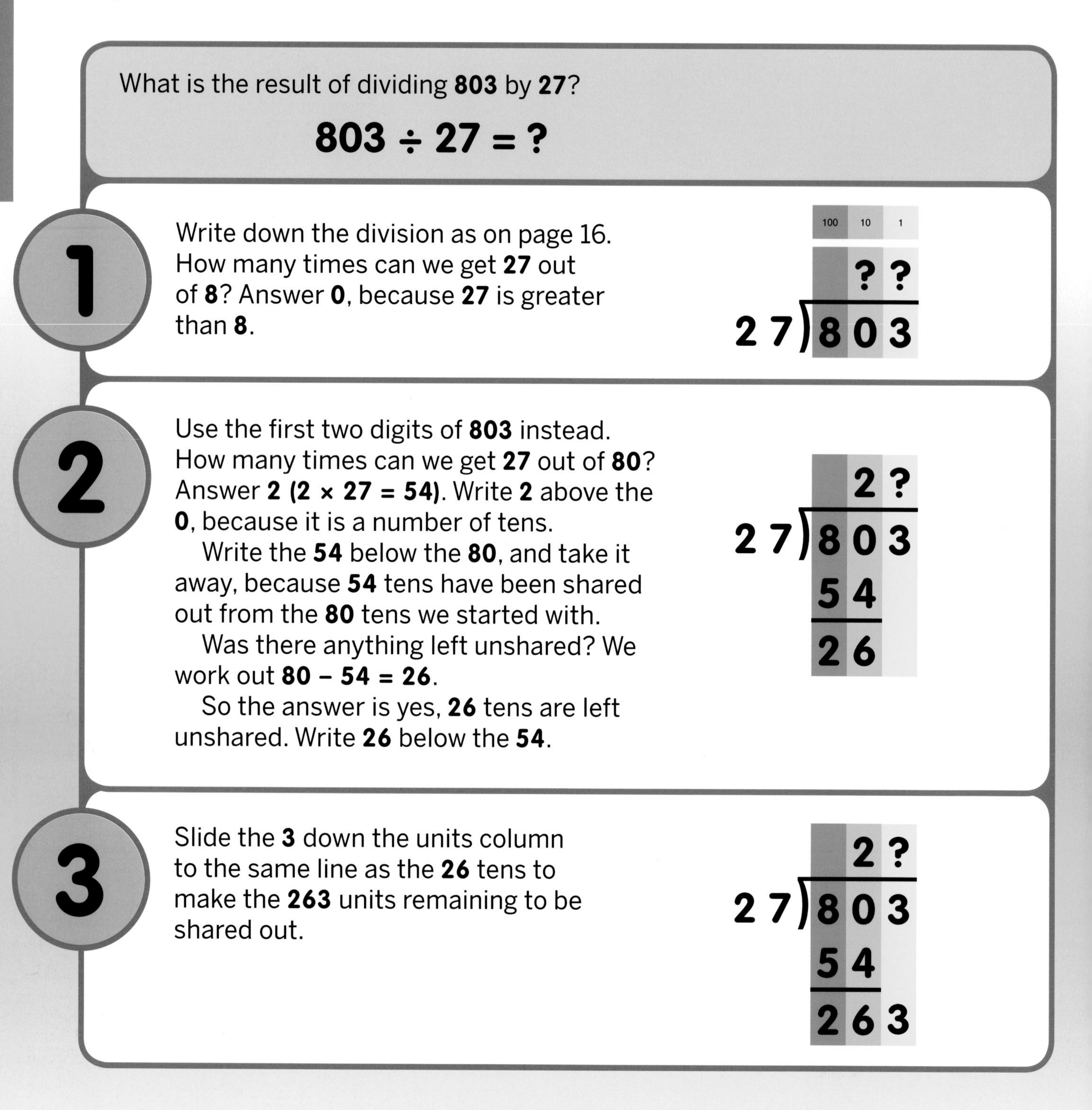

What is the result of dividing **803** by **27**?

$$803 \div 27 = ?$$

1

Write down the division as on page 16. How many times can we get **27** out of **8**? Answer **0**, because **27** is greater than **8**.

2

Use the first two digits of **803** instead. How many times can we get **27** out of **80**? Answer **2 (2 × 27 = 54)**. Write **2** above the **0**, because it is a number of tens.

Write the **54** below the **80**, and take it away, because **54** tens have been shared out from the **80** tens we started with.

Was there anything left unshared? We work out **80 − 54 = 26**.

So the answer is yes, **26** tens are left unshared. Write **26** below the **54**.

3

Slide the **3** down the units column to the same line as the **26** tens to make the **263** units remaining to be shared out.

Remember... There is often a remainder after a long division. This remainder could be written as a fraction, which in this example would be $^{20}/_{27}$. The remainder could also be written as a decimal.

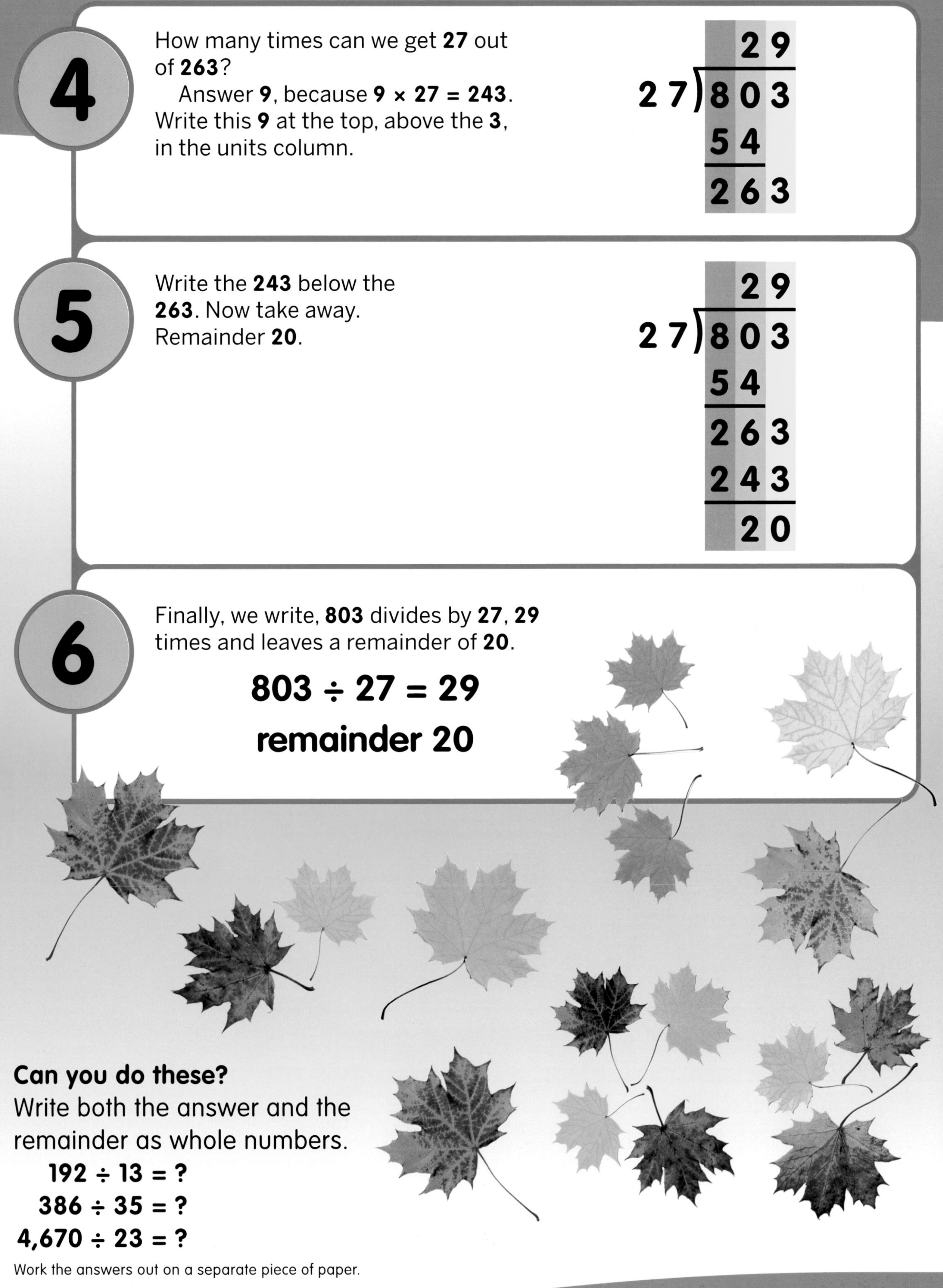

4

How many times can we get **27** out of **263**?

Answer **9**, because **9 × 27 = 243**. Write this **9** at the top, above the **3**, in the units column.

```
      29
27 ) 803
     54
     263
```

5

Write the **243** below the **263**. Now take away. Remainder **20**.

```
      29
27 ) 803
     54
     263
     243
      20
```

6

Finally, we write, **803** divides by **27**, **29** times and leaves a remainder of **20**.

803 ÷ 27 = 29

remainder 20

Can you do these?

Write both the answer and the remainder as whole numbers.

192 ÷ 13 = ?

386 ÷ 35 = ?

4,670 ÷ 23 = ?

Work the answers out on a separate piece of paper.

Division with decimal numbers

Decimal numbers are whole numbers and parts of whole numbers. The parts of a number are to the right of the decimal point.

It is much easier to divide by a whole number than by a decimal, so we arrange things to make the number we are dividing by into a whole number.

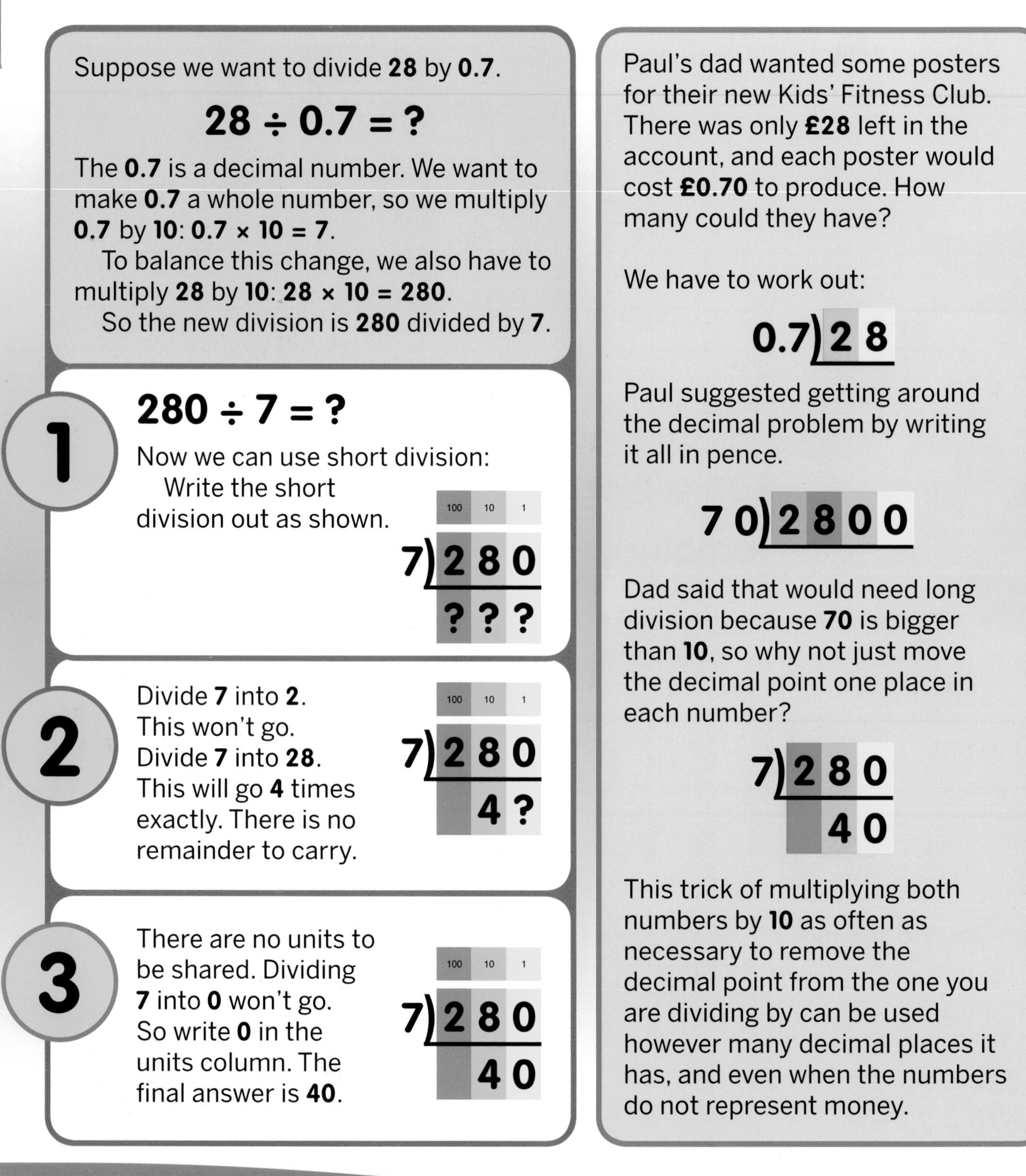

Suppose we want to divide **28** by **0.7**.

$$28 \div 0.7 = ?$$

The **0.7** is a decimal number. We want to make **0.7** a whole number, so we multiply **0.7** by **10**: **0.7 × 10 = 7**.

To balance this change, we also have to multiply **28** by **10**: **28 × 10 = 280**.

So the new division is **280** divided by **7**.

1

$$280 \div 7 = ?$$

Now we can use short division:

Write the short division out as shown.

	100	10	1
7)	2	8	0
	?	?	?

2

Divide **7** into **2**. This won't go. Divide **7** into **28**. This will go **4** times exactly. There is no remainder to carry.

	100	10	1
7)	2	8	0
		4	?

3

There are no units to be shared. Dividing **7** into **0** won't go. So write **0** in the units column. The final answer is **40**.

	100	10	1
7)	2	8	0
		4	0

Paul's dad wanted some posters for their new Kids' Fitness Club. There was only **£28** left in the account, and each poster would cost **£0.70** to produce. How many could they have?

We have to work out:

0.7) 2 8

Paul suggested getting around the decimal problem by writing it all in pence.

7 0) 2 8 0 0

Dad said that would need long division because **70** is bigger than **10**, so why not just move the decimal point one place in each number?

7)	2	8	0
		4	0

This trick of multiplying both numbers by **10** as often as necessary to remove the decimal point from the one you are dividing by can be used however many decimal places it has, and even when the numbers do not represent money.

Dividing decimals of different lengths

Sometimes the decimal numbers in a division have different lengths. For example: **547.96 ÷ 9.5**. Multiply both numbers by the same number of **10's** until the number you are dividing by is a whole number. Multiply both numbers by **10**. This changes **9.5** to **95**, a whole number and **547.96** to **5,479.6**. Notice that the number we are dividing into is still a decimal number. However, this won't cause any trouble.

547.96 ÷ 9.5 = ?

is the same as

5,479.6 ÷ 95 = ?

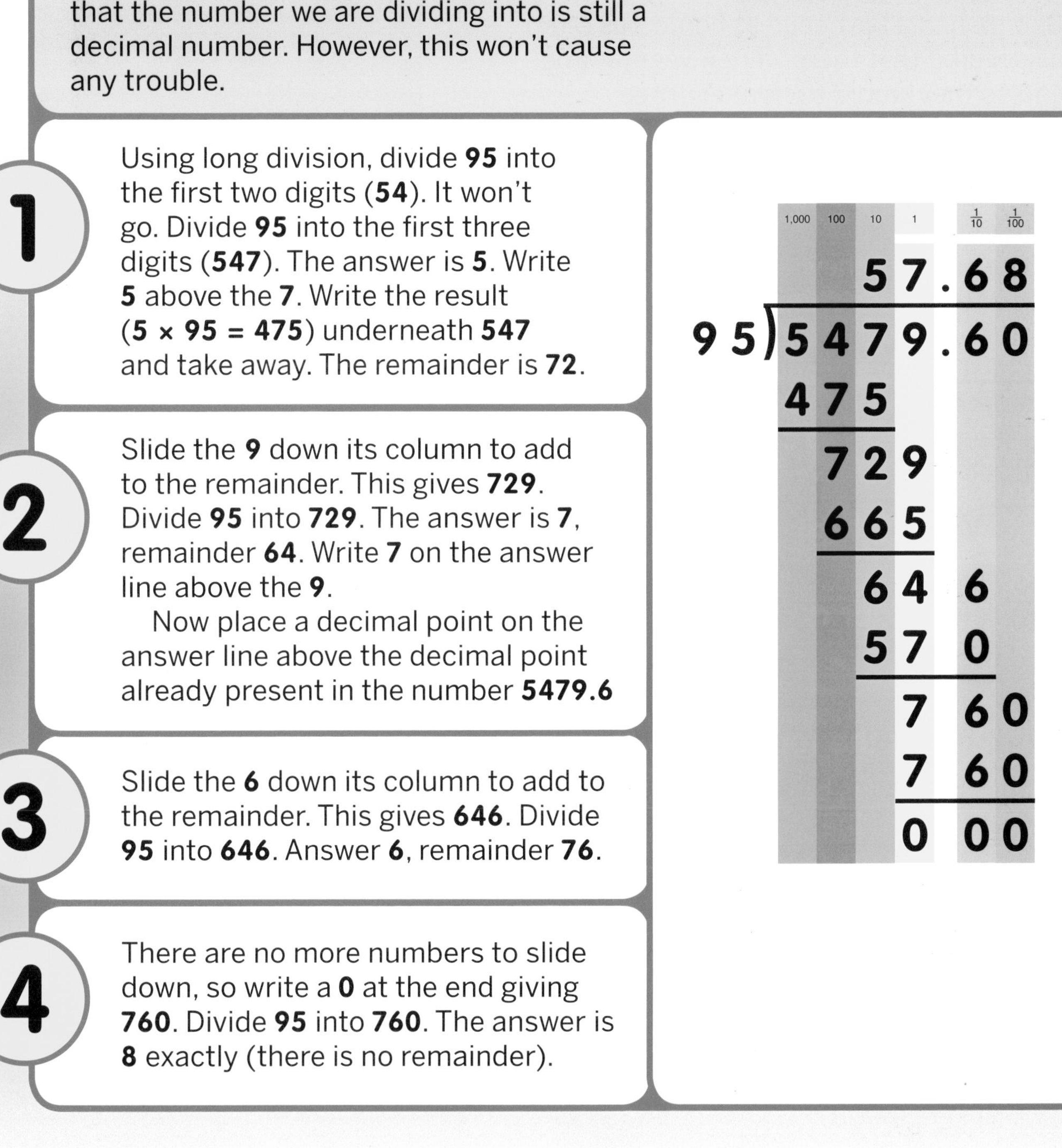

1 Using long division, divide **95** into the first two digits (**54**). It won't go. Divide **95** into the first three digits (**547**). The answer is **5**. Write **5** above the **7**. Write the result (**5 × 95 = 475**) underneath **547** and take away. The remainder is **72**.

2 Slide the **9** down its column to add to the remainder. This gives **729**. Divide **95** into **729**. The answer is **7**, remainder **64**. Write **7** on the answer line above the **9**.

Now place a decimal point on the answer line above the decimal point already present in the number **5479.6**

3 Slide the **6** down its column to add to the remainder. This gives **646**. Divide **95** into **646**. Answer **6**, remainder **76**.

4 There are no more numbers to slide down, so write a **0** at the end giving **760**. Divide **95** into **760**. The answer is **8** exactly (there is no remainder).

Can you do these?

42 ÷ 0.6 = ?

65.72 ÷ 3.1 = ?

Work the answers out on a separate piece of paper.

Remember... To divide whole numbers into decimals, you can use either short or long division.

Using remainders

Remainders can sometimes be used sensibly. Here you will also see when the answer is best shown as a fraction.

The barbecue

George had a barbecue at home. His Mum discovered that there were **4** vegetarians, and so they would each need three vegetarian burgers instead of the steaks that everyone else was eating.

Unfortunately, they only had **11** vegetarian burgers.

The problem they had to solve was how to share **11** between **4**. In other words they had to find out how many times **4** can be shared out of **11**? They got out the plates to find the answer and discovered that it was **2** each, but there were still **3** burgers remaining; that is, three were left over.

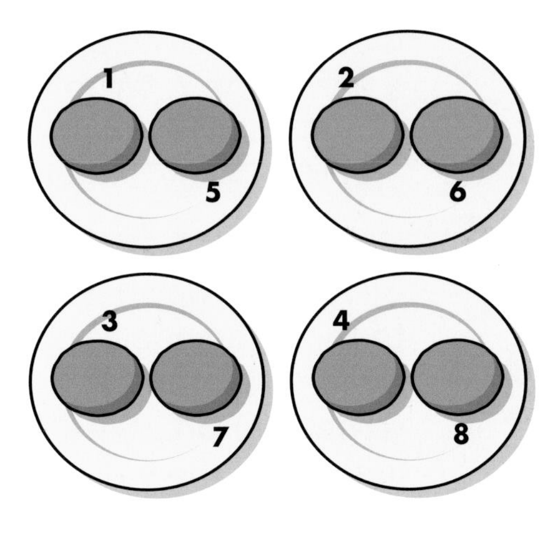

$11 \div 4 = 2$, remainder 3

The remainder can be written as $\frac{3}{4}$

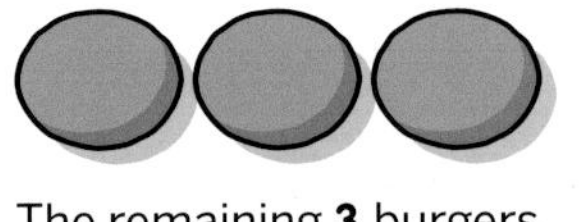

The remaining **3** burgers

What use is the remainder?

In this case it was best to use all the burgers, so they divided the remaining burgers among the guests (giving each an extra $^3/_4$), thus putting **2 + $^3/_4$** of a burger on each plate.

Thirsty play

Four friends were playing together in the garden one hot afternoon. The mother of one of them came out with a large jug of fruit juice that would fill **6** glasses.

$6 \div 4 = ?$

She filled a glass for each child and put the partly-empty jug on the table. This meant that there were **2** glasses-worth of juice remaining in the jug.

$6 \div 4 = 1$, remainder 2

The remainder

The remainder can be written as $2/4$, which on dividing top and bottom by two becomes $1/2$.

Sharing the remaining juice equally means that each of the friends receives the remainder as a very welcome half a glass-worth.

Remainder 2 is $\frac{2}{4}$ or $\frac{1}{2}$

Emily, Madison and Olivia were thirsty on the way home from netball. They had only one bottle of mineral water between them. Instead of doing the division **$1 \div 3 = 0$** remainder **1**, which would mean nothing for each girl and a full bottle remaining, they sensibly shared the one bottle between three girls and drank $1/3$ of it each.

Remember... A remainder is often most sensibly expressed as a fraction. In these examples you will see that $3/4$ of a burger or $1/2$ a glass is easy to share out.

Can you do this? Deepak has **£8** pocket money each week. What is the best way to share it out equally between each day, with a bit extra for Saturday?

Work the answer out on a separate piece of paper.

Value for money

Many stores sell goods in large bags or in multiple packs. But do you get better value with these than when you buy small packs or single items?

Josh wondered if he could save the family money by buying some large packs of breakfast cereal to take home.

Large cereal test

One brand was sold in packs of **48**, or **24** or **12** cereal bars.

The **48** pack cost **£3.04**.

The **24** pack cost **£1.59**.

And the **12** pack was on special offer at **98** pence.

One way to find out which size pack gives the best value is to calculate how much you pay for one cereal bar. To do this you have to find the price and divide it by the number of bars in the pack.

So Josh did this for each of the three packs.

For the **48** pack he worked out:

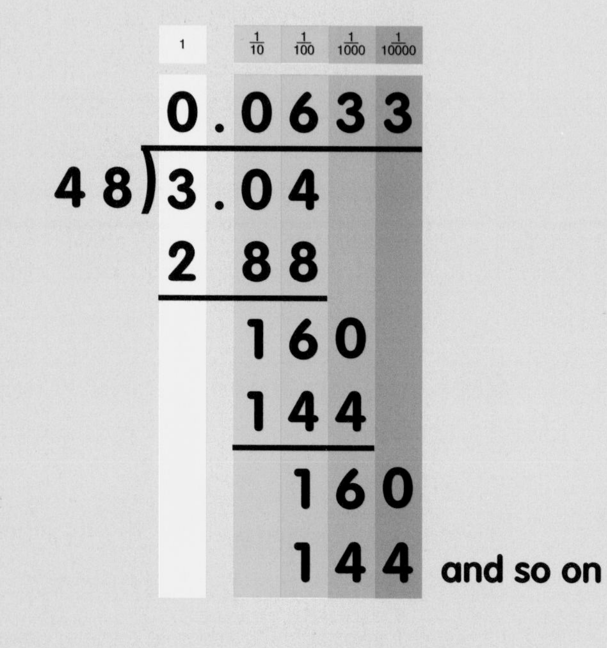

For the **24** pack he worked out:

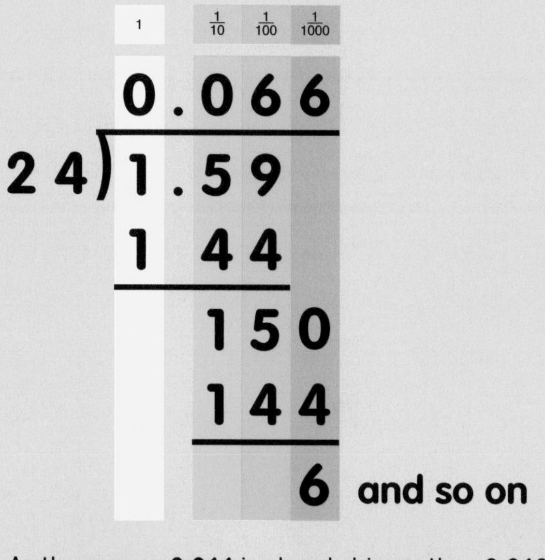

As the answer **0.066** is already bigger than **0.0633**, Josh can stop dividing now because it does not matter what happens next.

For the **12** pack he worked out:

That was already enough to decide it.

The small, special offer pack worked out at over **8** pence for one bar.

The bigger packs, which were not on offer, were almost the same as each other at over **6** pence for one bar. If you needed a lot, the **48** pack would be better value. But if some of them would go stale and be wasted, it was almost as good value to buy **24**.

Multipack smoothie test

Josh also liked fruit smoothies. He found these.

Kids' smoothies apple & blackcurrant
1 litre carton **£3.14**, buy two for **£5**
6-pack of **180 ml** bottles **£3.99**

Josh needed to know how much each (say) **100 ml** cost. For the **6-pack** he worked out **6 x 180 = 1,080 ml = 10.8 lots of 100 ml.**

So **100 ml** would cost **3.99 ÷ 10.8 = 39.9 ÷ 108:**

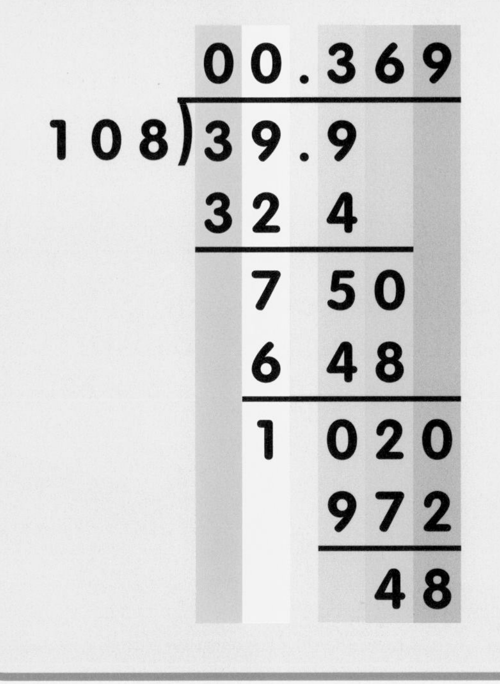

That means **100 ml** bought this way costs over **£0.369**, or **36.9 pence**.

A **1 litre** carton costs **£3.14**.
That is **£3.14 ÷ 10 = £0.314**, or **31.4 pence**, for **100 ml.**
And two of them cost **£5**, which is **£2.50** each.
That is **£2.50 ÷ 10 = £0.25**, or **25 pence**, for **100 ml.**

If Josh wants to buy about a litre, the single carton is better value than the **6-pack**.
If he wants more than a litre, the offer of **£5** for two is the best buy.

Can you do these? A six-pack of cat food costs **£3.29**. But there is a "buy 2 cans get one free" offer for only **£1.65**. You want six cans. What is it best to do? What would you do if you wanted 9 cans?

Work the answers out on a separate piece of paper.

Remember... You often need to know which item is the best value. To do this you have to find out how much they cost for the same weight, size, etc.

Fractional parts

Fractions are parts of a whole that use a horizontal line to show division.

We all go off to the zoo

The whole school is going on an outing by bus to the zoo. The bus company has big buses, which can each take $1/4$ of the school, and small buses, which can each take $1/6$ of the school.

On the day of the outing the bus company discovered it could only spare three big buses that day, though it had plenty of smaller ones. So how many buses should they provide?

They began thinking of three big buses and two small ones:

Three big buses would take $3 \times \frac{1}{4} = \frac{3}{4}$ of the school.

Two small buses would take $2 \times \frac{1}{6} = \frac{2}{6}$ of the school.

Adding these fractions together $\frac{3}{4} + \frac{2}{6} = ?$

To add fractions, the bottom numbers have to be the same. Since $3/4$ has a bottom number of **4**, and $2/6$ has a bottom number of **6**, the easiest way to make the fractions the same kind is to convert them both to **24ths**, because **4 × 6 = 24**.

$$= \frac{18}{24} + \frac{8}{24} = \frac{26}{24}$$

(18 = 3 x 6, 24 = 4 x 6; 8 = 2 x 4, 24 = 6 x 4)

The whole school is, of course, $^{24}/_{24}$ths. Since $^{3}/_{4} + ^{2}/_{6} = ^{26}/_{24}$, there would be empty seats this way. So would it help to use only two big buses and three small ones?

$$2 \times \frac{1}{4} + 3 \times \frac{1}{6}$$

$$= \frac{2}{4} + \frac{3}{6}$$

$$= \frac{12}{24} + \frac{12}{24}$$

(numerators: 2 x 6, 3 x 4; denominators: 4 x 6, 6 x 4)

$$= \frac{24}{24}$$

That takes exactly the right number of children.

You can subtract fractional parts in a similar way.

Lizzie topped up the screenwash in the family car. She could see from the markings on the bottle that the bottle was $^{3}/_{4}$ full when she started, and only $^{1}/_{12}$ full at the end. Lizzie wanted to work out what fraction of a bottleful the car took, so that she would know for next time.

Lizzie works it out like this.

$^{3}/_{4} - ^{1}/_{12}$

$= ^{9}/_{12} - ^{1}/_{12}$

$= ^{8}/_{12}$

$= ^{2}/_{3}$

Can you do this? If only one big bus was available, why might it have been better not to use it?

Give your answer out on a separate piece of paper.

Remember... To add fractions, the bottoms must be made the same. Once they are, just add the tops.

Fractions with the same value

Fractions can be written in several ways while having the same value.

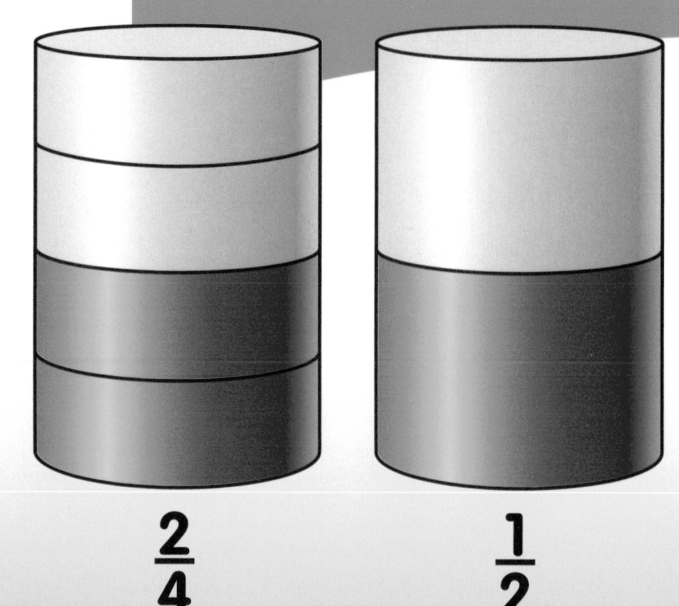

We write half of something as $^1/_2$. It is actually **1** divided by **2**. But a half is also the same as two quarters ($^2/_4$, two divided by four).

Because these two fractions represent the same amount, we say that they are equivalent fractions (equivalent means 'the same').

In this example notice that the numbers **2** and **4** both divide exactly by **2**, so if you divide both the top and bottom of $^2/_4$ by **2**, you get $^1/_2$. This proves that $^2/_4$ has the same value as $^1/_2$.

Making mp3 players

In a factory making mp3 players the first-stage machine makes **15** pieces an hour. So each one takes **$^1/_{15}$th** of an hour. The second-stage machine works at only **12** pieces an hour. So each one takes **$^1/_{12}$th** of an hour.

This is how to work out how long it takes to make each mp3 player.

The total time to make each mp3 player is therefore **$^1/_{15}$th + $^1/_{12}$th** of an hour. So we need to work out:

$$\frac{1}{15} + \frac{1}{12} = ?$$

1

To add these fractions, we need to convert each fraction so that both have the same bottom numbers. See how both **15** and **12** will divide into **60**, and so we now multiply the top and bottom of this fraction by **4**.

We then multiply the top and bottom of this fraction by **5**.

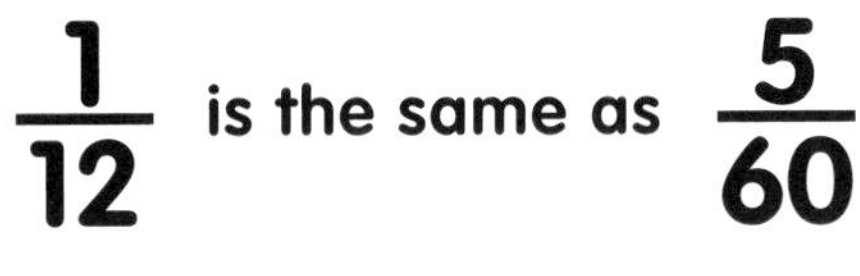

Now the fractions have the same bottom numbers we can add them.

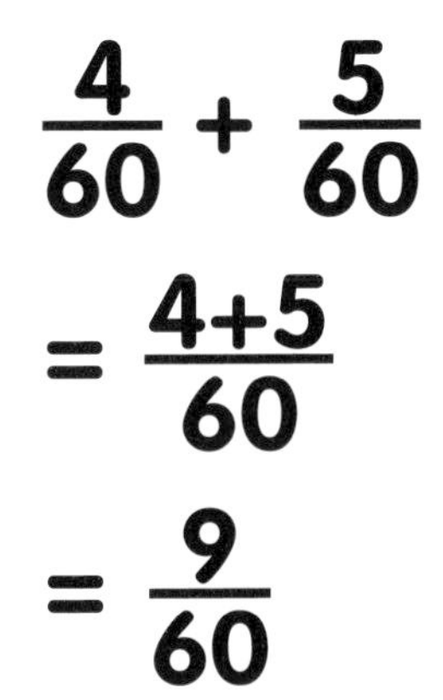

Each mp3 takes $^9/_{60}$**ths** of an hour, or **9** minutes to be made.

This is a way to get the bottom numbers the same.

Multiply top and bottom by **2**, then by **3**, then by **4** and so on.

$$\frac{1}{6} = \frac{2}{12} = \frac{3}{18} = \frac{4}{24} = \frac{5}{30}$$

These are equivalent fractions.

$$\frac{1}{8} = \frac{2}{16} = \frac{3}{24} = \frac{4}{32} = \frac{5}{40}$$

These are equivalent fractions, too.

So the fractions $^1/_6$ and $^1/_8$ each have an equivalent fraction with a matching bottom number – $^4/_{24}$ and $^3/_{24}$.

This first possible matching bottom number is called the lowest common denominator. So the lowest common denominator of **6** and **8** is **24**. This is the smallest number **6** and **8** will both divide into exactly. Using this information you can work out the answer:

$$\frac{1}{6} - \frac{1}{8} = \frac{4}{24} - \frac{3}{24} = \frac{1}{24}$$

You could use **6 x 8 = 48**. It is a common denominator, but it is not the lowest.

Using the lowest common denominator (LCD, for short) makes the maths easier.

Remember... Always look for the smallest number to use at the bottoms of the fractions. In this case both **12** and **15** go into **60**. Similarly, if you had fractions with bottoms of **6** and **8**, then you could use **6 × 8 = 48**, but both numbers will also go into **24**, and this is a smaller and so better number to work with.

Can you do these?

$^1/_4 + {}^5/_6 = ?$

$^1/_8 - {}^1/_{10} = ?$

Work the answers out on a separate piece of paper.

Per is a word for divide

Per is a common shorthand meaning 'for each' or 'has already been divided'.

If a student receives an exam mark of **60** per cent (written **60%**), it means that the teacher has worked out the grade as a fraction of **100** (**$^{60}/_{100}$ths**). Here is another example.

Can Hilary get the job?

Hilary wanted to be a secretary. This meant that she must be able to type **80** words per minute.

She worried that the speed might be checked at an interview, so to be confident, she thought she would check it for herself. She began to type at her keyboard. She used a timer to time herself for **15** minutes. Hilary then counted the number of words she had typed: **1,284**. So what was her typing speed?

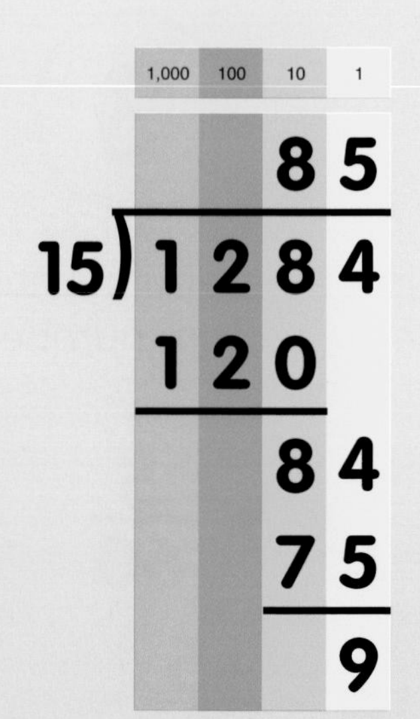

1,284 words in 15 minutes is
1,284 ÷ 15 words for each minute

or $\frac{1,284}{15}$ words per minute

= 85 (and a bit) words per minute – easily enough for the job!

Jacob drove out of Birmingham at **10** miles per hour for half an hour, then at **60** miles per hour for another one and a half hours on the M6. What was his speed overall?

In the first $\frac{1}{2}$ hour, Jacob covered **10 x** $\frac{1}{2}$ **= 5** miles. In the second hour and a half he covered **60 x** $1\frac{1}{2}$ **= 90** miles (because **60 x 1 = 60** and **60 x** $\frac{1}{2}$ **= 30**). Overall he travelled **5 + 90 = 95** miles in two hours, so his speed was...

$$2\overline{)9\,{}^{1}5\,.\,{}^{1}0}$$
$$47.5$$

... that is **47**$\frac{1}{2}$ miles per hour, or miles in one hour.

Notice that his speed is not half way between **10 mph** and **60 mph** (which would be **35 mph**) because he spent more time on the M6.

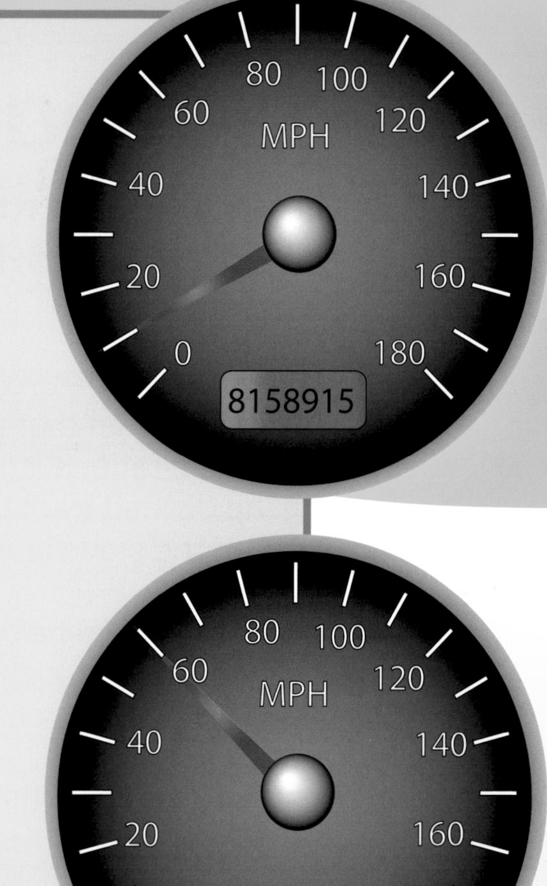

Estimating before calculating

If you use your calculator instead of long division how do you then know that you have not made a mistake while pressing the keys? Make a rough guess at the answer before you use the calculator.

For example, Hilary typed **1,284** words in **15** minutes, which is approximately **1,300** in **15** minutes. This is approximately **100** words per minute.

Now that we have a rough estimate, we can compare it with a calculator.

Use your calculator...

1. Enter **1,284**
2. Press division sign (÷ or /)
3. Enter **15**
4. Press equals sign (=)

(Answer reads **85.6**)

Can you do these?

300 miles covered by a lorry in **6** hours is **?** miles per hour.
3,900 miles covered by a plane in **7.5** hours is **?** mph.

Work the answers out on a separate piece of paper.

Remember... In some cases the remainder is not important. Learn when to ignore it.

In can mean divide

'In' sometimes means a ratio, which is another way of saying divide.

If you come to a steep hill, the chances are you see a warning sign that uses the word 'in'. This is a ratio. It is another way of writing 'up divided by along'.

You can think of the slope as a kind of imaginary staircase.

The slope in the diagram below is matched by a staircase in which the length of the treads (**1** unit) equals the height of the risers (**1** unit). So for every step up or down the staircase, you go as far up or down as you do on the level.

This can be written down as

1 in 1

but it can also be written as

1 : 1 (a ratio)

It is also the fraction

$$\frac{1}{1}$$

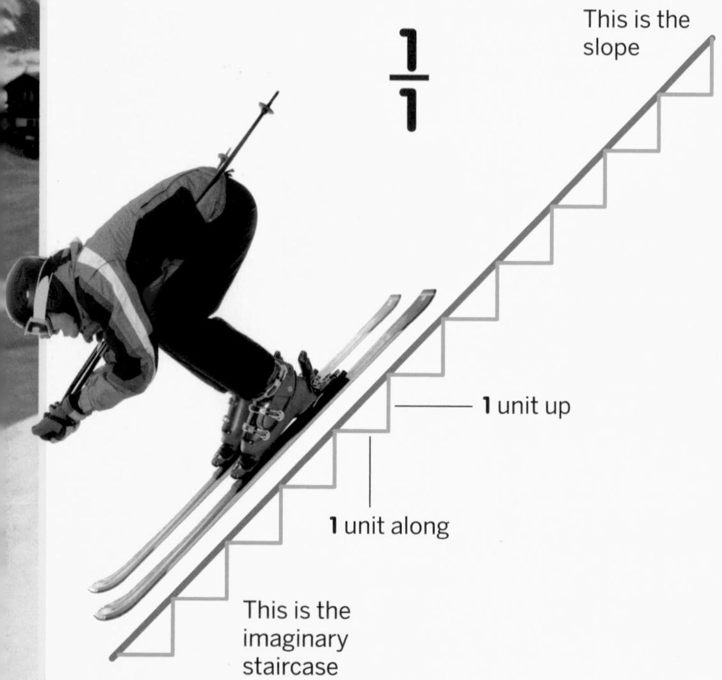

This is the slope

1 unit up

1 unit along

This is the imaginary staircase

2 units up

6 units along

If the slope is **2** up for every **6** along, the slope is

2 in 6

Dividing through by **2** this simplifies to

1 in 3

or

1 : 3

or the fraction

$$\frac{1}{3}$$

This is less steep.

How steep is the roller coaster?

Some friends were about to go on a roller coaster. The information boards said: greatest drop **235** feet, speed reached **70** miles an hour, horizontal distance covered **125** feet.

The up or down distance is **235** feet. The across distance is **125** feet. We need to work out how far across the roller coaster goes for every **1** foot down. That means dividing by **235**. You could do it by long division, but (once you have clearly decided what you need to work out) it is much easier to use a calculator (see below).

The slope is **1 in 0.53** or **1 : 0.53**

Notice that **1 in 1** is steeper than **1 in 3**, and **1 in 0.53** is steeper still.

Remember... These special forms of division replace the division line by the word 'in' or a colon (:). That is why **1 : 2** is steeper than **1 : 3**.

Use your calculator...

1. Enter **125**
2. Press division sign (÷ or /)
3. Enter **235**
4. Press equals sign (=)

(Answer reads **0.5319148**. **0.53** will be near enough)

Can you do this? Arrange these slopes in order of steepness, with the steepest first.

Steep incline for a train	**1 in 100**
Road hill at Porlock	**1 in 3**
Motorway hill	**1 in 40**
Steep hill on a bike	**1 in 10**
Snowdon mountain railway	**1 in 8**

Write out the answer on a separate piece of paper.

Solving division equations

Here you can see how we use division to find an unknown amount in an equation.

Fancy chocolates

Kevin has been out to buy **20** fancy chocolates to eat. His mother wanted two. The others were shared equally between Kevin and his **5** friends.

He does not know how many chocolates each person will have. He works it out like this, using the letter **C** for the number of chocolates per person.

Suppose everybody apart from Mother has **C** chocolates.

We know that **6** (people) **×** **C** (number each) **+** **2** (for mother) make up the **20** chocolates. This can be written as:

People Chocolates Mother Total bought

$$6 \times C + 2 = 20$$

So the problem is to find how many chocolates **C** represents.

Remember, if you do the same to both sides of an equation, you don't change the equation.

$$6 \times C + 2 - 2 = 20 - 2$$

$$6 \times C = 18$$

Divide both sides by **6**

$$C = 3$$

Maria has bought five basketballs for the Kids' Fitness Club. She had a voucher for **£12** off any purchase. Paul's dad wants to know how much each ball cost. Maria can only remember that she paid **£128** altogether. This is how they worked it out.

Use the letter **C** for the cost of one basketball.

$$5 \times C - 12 = 128$$

Add **12** to each side of our equation.

$$5 \times C - 12 + 12 = 128 + 12$$

Or simply

$$5 \times C = 140$$

Now divide each side of the new equation by **5**.

$$5 \div 5 \times C = 140 \div 5$$

$$C = 140 \div 5$$

$$C = 28$$

$$5\overline{)1\,4\,{}^{4}0}$$
$$\quad 2\,8$$

The shop price of each basketball was **£28**.

Can you do this?
Maria remembered it wrongly. She really paid **£138** altogether. What is the correct shop price for each basketball?

Work the answer out on a separate piece of paper.

Remember... To check your answer. It is always worth looking for a way to check that the answer is correct. A good way is to put the answers back into the question to check that they work. Here, **6** people each take **3** chocolates, making **18**. Mother takes **2**. So the total chocolates = **20**, which is correct.

What symbols mean

Here is a list of the common maths symbols together with an example of how they are used.

+ The symbol for adding. We say it 'plus'. In Latin plus means 'more'.

− Between two numbers this symbol means 'subtract' or 'minus'. In front of one number it means the number is a minus number. In Latin minus means 'less'.

= The symbol for equals. We say it 'equals' or 'makes'. It comes from a Latin word meaning 'level' because weighing scales are level when the amounts on each side are equal.

$$(8 + 9 - 3) \times \frac{2}{5} = 5.6$$

( ) The symbols for brackets. You do everything inside the brackets first. Brackets always occur in pairs.

× The symbol for multiplying. We say it 'multiplied by' or 'times'.

—, **/** and **÷** Three symbols for dividing. We say it 'divided by'. A pair of numbers above and below a **/** or **—** make a fraction, so **2/5** or $\frac{2}{5}$ is the fraction two-fifths.

• This is a decimal point. It is a dot written after the units when a number contains parts of a unit as well as whole numbers. This is the decimal number five point six.

Index